MW00329013

The Art of Harmony

A Book of Freedom from Within

The Art of Harmony

by
Sang H. Kim

Turtle Press ● Hartford

THE ART OF HARMONY

Copyright © 1994 Sang H. Kim. All rights reserved. Printed in United States of America. No part of this book may be used or reproduced without written permission except in the case of brief quotations embodied in articles or reviews. To contact the author or to order additional copies of this book: Turtle Press, P. O. Box 290206, Wethersfield, CT 06129-0206.

Library of Congress Card Catalog Number

ISBN 1-880336-03-0　　　　　　First Edition

Library of Congress Cataloguing in Publication Data
Kim, Sang H.
　　　　The art of harmony / by Sang H. Kim - - 1st ed.
　　　　　　　　p.　　cm.
　　　　ISBN 1-880336-03-0 : $6.95
　　　　1. Life -- Quotations, maxims, etc. 2. Harmony (philosophy) --Quoatations,
　　　　maxims, etc. 3. Self-realization --Quotations, maxims, etc.　I. Title.
　　BD435K444　1994
　　　158--dc20

　　　　　　　　　　　　　　　　　　　　　　93-43077

Preface

When I was in my twenties, I served for several years as a counter espionage agent near the truce line of North and South Korea. It was a time of intense pressure and often life-threatening danger. At the end of my service, I returned to my friends and family to find that nothing would ever again be the same. Their day-to-day cares and worries seemed trivial compared to the extremes of humanity I had just experienced. Life suddenly seemed mundane and aimless. There was no fulfillment, no challenge, no peace, no meaning.

With the hope of finding myself once more, I entered a Buddhist temple and undertook a forty day fast to purify my mind and body. During the first week of the fast I discovered how hungry I had been. The second week, how weak my body was. The third, how awful the smells were. The fourth, the blueness of the sky, the rhythmical sound of the ants crawling under my blanket. By the fifth week, nothing mattered. Everything flowed in its own pace and course, all are independent and unique, nothing meaningless. At last, peace! Amazingly, the peace came from the surrender of "Me." It was within me all the time, yet I could not see it until I abandoned all wants and desires.

Life itself comes from truth, the truth we experience as the innocence of childhood. However, as we mature, we discover the existence of life and death, which causes us to question the reason for our being. To escape the discord these questions bring, we must detach ourselves from the concepts of living and dying, conflict and peace, success and failure, hope and despair. When we abandon our attachments, we move toward freedom from ourselves and create space in our mind for happiness and fulfillment. When we are truly fulfilled, we are secure enough to open ourselves to the infinite wisdom of our world. From wisdom, comes harmony within ourselves and with our surroundings.

Life, I think, is not something that we can understand, but that we must accept and believe in. If we look beyond the chaos of each moment, we cannot help but see that we are but one glorious thread in the cloth of life.

Chapter 1: Truth

Truth

The only way to close the distance between our being
and pure objective reality
is to free ourselves for a moment.

Attainment

An effort to attain nothing
is the secret to attain everything.

~ ❖ ~

Being

Everything really is
only in our mind.

The ocean

Do not look after the truth,
but let the truth come in.

~ ~

Acceptance

It is very true that the truth itself
is not always applied equally in life.

The best time

Time brought us where we are now.
It will take us to where we came from.
There is no need to be in a hurry
because we are in a boat that sails at its own pace.

Impermanence

No moment lasts forever.
We only experience the process.
No lasting security exists.

Break the door

Every moment is an endless process of choices,
Choices into a wide variety of experiences.
When locked into preconceptions of how things look,
we are locked out from new and different possibilities.

Time

We occupy a space in time,
the space that cannot be measured by our eyes,
the time that can be dimly comprehended by us.

~ ~

Perseverance

No problem endures the passing of time.

Reunion

Nothing separates us from the rest but ourselves.
The separation makes a prison of our own,
confining us
in the optical illusion of our consciousness.
For a reunion, we must break down the fence
and embrace all beings with impartial compassion.

The door

The opportunity of happiness
always waits for us outside the door.
The misfortune of most of us
is that our attention is focused on the door itself.
The door is the thing that we must abandon
to go out to the new world.

Enjoy the noise

Time washes things off and equalizes.
Some time all of us will be in perfect silence and peace
so let's enjoy the hustle and bustle till the time.

Harmony

Harmony unfolds itself
when we release ourselves
from our own opinions
and experience our total being in unison.

Noble thing

Unity of self is the most noble thing to attain.
That is the bottomless spring of
love, generosity, and compassion.

Original mind

The original mind is a perfect mind,
the perfectness of the oneness before separation.
It has no form but exists in every form.
No form, no duality, no mind, oneness.
The mind where everything arises from and returns to.

Sunglasses

Opinions are the sunglasses
that filter reality into our own sanctuary.
The more different glasses we have,
the more colorful the scenes become.
But reality is still reality.

Is the sky?

Ideas and opinions are clouding the view of the sky.
Is it blue?
Is it gray?
Isn't it pretty?
Is it going to be cloudy?
Whatever we say, the sky is.

What am I?

What I am is a continuity of the process
of the way I feel,
the way I see,
the way I hear,
the way I speak,
and how I do things.

Questions

Who is laughing when you laugh ?
Who is crying when you cry ?
Who is living when you live ?
Who is dying when you die ?
Why do you laugh ?
Why do you cry ?
Why do you live ?
Why do you die ?
The moment of understanding this
will be the moment I stop asking.

Chapter 2: Life and death

Inspiration

If art is an inspiration,
life is a sentiment.

Wishing well

Life is a string of time.
It is being held down into the abyss
by the rope of the past.

Cloth of life

Life is a process of weaving mysterious threads
that link us to one another
and produce infinite memories of the journey.

One way path

It's a one way road.
No way to retreat, so keep walking on
straight and winding,
up and down,
hills and valleys.
Slow but steady.
We'll never be here again.

Live here

Every moment has a relationship to the next.
The effect of the previous moment
causes the rising of the next.
Life without this moment never exists.
It is only here at this moment.
Nothing more, nothing less.

Ride it

Things arise and things pass away.
Whatever comes, comes with the current,
nothing special to hold on to,
but riding on it.

Drive-in movie

The true being is a big void.
Like the big screen in the drive-in movie
on which scenes are projected.
Because of the emptiness, things can appear.
Without it, there is no space for anything to be shown.
After all of the joy and tears,
leaving the empty screen and the parking lot behind,
one must leave with only the memories.
Life, seems to me, like a series of movies.
I can see, laugh, cry, and enjoy things on the screen,
but there is nothing left to take with me but the illusion.

The peak

All beings pass through
the peak and decline of their season.

Life and death

Nothing binds us to the wheel of the life and death
but the clinging mind itself.

Changes

Death
Storms
Birth
Fortune
Karma
Have changed the world for millions of years.
Even at this moment we are influenced by them,
but they themselves never change.
We live and die,
its just a small part of the changes.
What's the big deal ?

The spirit

It is the possession of a body
that is the greatest hindrance to the spiritual life.

~ ~

The answer

Do not look for the answer
but the process.

Past, present, future

When we were born, life started.
With life, a force began to move.
When we felt the force our eyes opened,
the opening created a new world.
The world with a bright light.
The world with a dark shadow.
It is a world with two phenomena,
but the world is one world.

When the life force began,
the force split us in three directions.
The direction of the past, the present and the future.

The only reason for the being of the past
and the future is the present.
The force is alive only for the present moment.
The life of the past is dead.
The life of the future is only in our imagination.
The dead and the imagination are an illusion.
They are just the shadows of the present.

The past brings us sufferings and nostalgia.
The future brings us worries and hope.
Sufferings, nostalgia, worries and hope all are illusion.
They exist but in our mind.

Past, present, future (II)

The art of the harmony is the way of clearing illusions.
Not to shatter our spirit in two directions,
but one,
not to stretch out toward other directions,
but one.

To live fully.
To live dynamically.
To live with a clear mind.
To live with a higher spirit.
To live in one being and to become one.

The one where we came from.
The one where we are.
The one where we will return.
The one that we are.
The Isness.
Is

Rebirth

Unless the seed of an apple dies after it has been sown,
it will never bring forth much fruit.

Walk on through the tunnel

Many pointed out the way,
but it is ourselves who must walk
through the tunnel of the life to the end.

The Wonder of Aloneness

When I wake up in the morning, I awake alone.
When I go to bed at night, I fall to sleep alone.
So was it when I was born,
and so will it be when I die.
It took a while to come to know that aloneness
and it took even longer to become comfortable
with the simple truth.
That single realization
has made every relationship such a wonder since.

Death

To free ourselves from the fear of the death
we must realize that the death in the future
exists simply in our thoughts of the present moment.

Peace

Death is not something new.
When the idea of "I" ceases to exist,
fear transforms into peace.

One Way

Life is one way sail.
Everyday is the only today.
Sail on or regret.

Chapter 3: Discord

Time

Time does not fly.
It drops into the abyss.

Sorrow

A song of melancholy rises from the troubled sorrow.
The one who heeds it is no one but a fool.

In the past

When the past invades the dimension of the present,
the present moment in which this life is lived
drifts vacantly into the future.

I killed yesterday

Yesterday's pain is today's agony.
Tomorrow's uncertainty overshadows today's agony.
So I kill yesterday.

Discard the shadow

Feelings are the shadow of the mind.
They appear in the mirror of the mind.
The mind itself projects the reflections of them.
Beside the mind itself, everything is just a shadow.
Keep the mind, but discard the shadow.

Illusion

The concept of the mind itself is always constant
but the reality of the mind changes.
At every moment a new mind is created and fades away.
There is neither the same mind nor the permanent mind.
Any permanence is an illusion.

Perception

It is our perception that places meanings in things.
Often meanings are irrelevant to reality.
Meanings are only in our mind that sees reality
through the filter called perception.

Change of perceptions

When your perception changes,
the rainy day becomes sunny.

No problems

We might feel happier with no problems
but I am afraid, then,
we might not need each other anymore.

Conflict

When we attach ourselves to specific things
we create conflicts of energy.
When we detach ourselves from things
we free ourselves from the conflicts.

Conflict

A conflict brings anxiety.
The anxiety causes stress.
The stress becomes a symptom.
The symptom kills.
Fix the cause of the conflict.

Effort

Effort is a foundation of all achievement.
No one can succeed without conscientious efforts.
All sages can point out the way
but we each must walk the road for ourselves.

Changing perspective

Obstacles are inspectors who test our determination.
Jealousy is a sign of recognition.
Plateaus are milestones indicating another peak nearby.
Depression is the pulling of the string of the bow.
Stress is an exit sign to a rest area.
All problems are just our perception.
Change your perspective.
The night becomes a day,
the day reveals the heavens.

Problem solving

When problems occur, stop being driven by them.
Change the pace on your own.
Then the problem is no longer a problem but
a wonderful opportunity to a see a newer possibility.

Drive for the corner

On encountering multiple opponents
you must drive them into the corner
and defeat them one by one.
With fiery determination, press them strongly.
If you run away, you will be exhausted.

Don't blame the screen

When the mirror shakes the reflection moves.
For clarity of view the mirror must be balanced.

Knowledge is power

Knowledge is power,
the power like the water,
the water that a cow drinks,
the drink that turns into milk.
Knowledge is power,
the power of the water,
the water that a snake drinks,
the drink that turns into poison.

Patience

When things get boring and doubtful
patience keeps our mind in balance.
With balance in the mind
we can wait until everything unfolds in a natural way.

Ram it head on

In a crisis,
driving is safer than being driven.
Hold on tight,
take a deep breath
and ram it head on.

Finding the self

The fool sits in the cave, staring at the shadows.
The wise man turns around and pursues the torch.

Chapter 4: Detachment

Treasure hunter

Stop looking for the treasure from far away,
wandering around the hill of diamonds.
The real diamonds are forever within ourselves.

Confrontation

Confronting the self honestly is the best way
to keep things in life clear and free of distractions.
Then all relationships resume to be simple and hap

Abandonment of self

To sail on the ocean,
one must not fear of leaving the harbor.
After crossing the river,
one must not doubt in abandoning the boat.
To enjoy the beauty of the moon,
one must not think of the pointing finger.
To understand one's life,
one must not fear of leaving the self.

Possession

If you want to achieve harmony,
you cannot have it.
Just believe in the way you are,
then you already have it.
Don't sacrifice the means for the end.

Deconditioning desire

The more we cling, the more burdens we accumulate.
To let things go is to keep the mind light.
We are mistakenly conditioned to possess.
When we let go of the desire, we create freedom within.

Strength

The toughest man
is the one who can sit quietly
with no mask.

Retreat for victory

Initial retreat
is intended to attain the ultimate victory
in the end.

Turn around to face the light

Concepts are the shadow of our true self.
Concepts fluctuate whenever the light changes.
They create ups and downs of the perception of things.
When we turn around facing the light,
there are no more shadows, no more concepts.

Me

"Me" is the vehicle of the experience of a life,
nothing more, nothing less.

Gravity

We would feel lighter with no gravity,
but we couldn't play basketball.

Doubt

While we had no idea of where we came from,
we were in perfect harmony with our world.
Once we started thinking of who we are,
the trouble started.

Illusive self

The word "self" stays the same
but the self is ever changing.
In meditation the concept of self disappears.
The nonconceptual level of being arises,
totally free of thought.
It is the experience of what is happening
rather than what we think of what is happening.

Empty mind

Mind is not a concept or thought.
It is just a vehicle
on which all thoughts and concepts appear
and fade away.

One thing

When we understand one thing thoroughly
we can understand many things as well.
When we try to understand everything at one time
there is nothing we can understand fully.
The first thing which must be understood most of all,
is yourself.

Reality vs. concepts

Reality is certain
but concepts are manipulative.
Reality is in constant flux
but concepts are static.
Reality is impermanent
but concepts are illusions of permanence.
We are experiencing reality
but confined by the chain of concepts.

3 soul burners

Wealth, fame and power
are the three fires that burn the soul.
Wealth burns the spirit of equality.
Fame burns the spirit of friendship.
Power burns the spirit of justice.

Greed

Greed and war are the most primary shame of humanity.
The shame is the loss of our naturalness.
When we are natural within,
then we are in harmony with others.
The loss of paradise was caused by no one but ourselves.

Possession

Possessive desire conditions the mind toward vanity.
No possession, no vanity.
Having without possessing is fulfillment without vanity.

Discipline

Discipline is the ability to do what must be done,
even when you don't feel like doing it.

Honesty

Whatever we learn we must start from where we are.
The starting point is from within us,
not outside of ourselves.

Strength

The loss of strength of one kind
can be replaced by a strength of another kind.
The acceptance of physical limitation
opens up the door to spiritual enlightenment.

Harmonize the force

When attacked,
harmonize yourself
with the tide of the opponent's brutal force.

Conditioned way

We are well conditioned to take whatever we want
therefore the tension and the disturbances are endless.
By deconditioning ourselves to give and let go
we can lessen the burden of our life.

Bondage

The body binds the mind within the bondage.
The mind has no way out but surrenders
because that is the only way out.

Clear mind

The mind is like a mirror
all things arise and pass away.
There is no special thing to hold on to.
Whatever comes in, let it come.
Whatever goes out, let it go.

Be yourself

When you are the way you are
you have so much space in your mind.
When you try to be somebody who you are not
you become easily threatened and defensive.
So be the way you are,
then the space will be full of peace and love.

Power

He who knows himself is the one who has the power.

Enslaved

When we believe in the shadows of ourselves
we are slaves chained in the dark cave.

放

Chapter 5: Freedom

The circle

When I am asleep,
all my life becomes free from a circle.
The circle that has surrounded me
with the chain of hours,
the sequence of the seasons,
and the order of the worldly habits.

Simplicity

In the haste of dashing to success
we sacrifice the time, energy and sustenance
to pursue more profound parts of our life.

Meditation

Meditation is a journey into the realm of our mind.
It's a silent exploration of who and what we are.
The discovery is a difficult process
but one of the most noble things to experience.

Naturalness

Be free to behold the deep sky in mid-autumn.
Be free to breath in the breeze of May.
Be free to smell the daisies in the meadow.
Be free to listen to the sparrows on the birch.
Most of all, be free to choose your one true self.

Fix this moment, improve the past

Every moment is a prerequisite for the rising of the next.
The accumulations of the past brought us to this moment.
The continuity of the process repeats for the next moment.
If we don't like this moment, we must fix it,
before it becomes another part of the accumulated past.

Imperfection

The red rose stands out on the leaves of green.
Among reds, it is just another red.
The imperfection is a light for the silhouette of harmony.

Let it go

If you truly want to win, forget winning.
If you truly want to gain, forget gaining.
If you truly want to love, forget receiving love.
Then you will find yourself having them all
in the middle of the great void.

Free your mind

If you look for freedom with a shackled mind
there is nothing like freedom.
If you look for freedom with a free mind,
full of freedom is the world.
Be free before you seek freedom.

Liberation

At the crossroad of life and death,
surrender is the exit into the bigger, quieter world.
Without surrender, the door can never be opened.

Tradition vs. freedom

There is no such a thing as an everlasting tradition.
Tradition started somewhere in the past, by somebody.
How we relate to what is happening at this moment
is more important than how this moment
can fit into the tradition of a century ago.
How to react to each moment
is very much within the freedom of each of us.

Free to choose

The art of the harmony is the way of freedom.
Accept the way things are,
see things as they are.
Let things arise from nothingness.
You are free to choose which course to take,
the path that will bring you the most joy of life.

福

Chapter 6: Happiness

Giving

Happiness comes when love is being shared.
Peace fills the corners of the heart
when the grip of desire is released.
Wisdom shines when the greed turns into generosity.

Cast away the ball

Cast away the ball.
The feeling afterward is the reason for having it.
Releasing the self is the reason for having it.

Stop chasing

Stop chasing after happiness.
The more you reach out, the further she flees.
Vacate the occupied mind, then it will be fully filled.

The rainbow

Happiness is a rainbow
that we can enjoy seeing but not grasp.

Joyful pond

No words for true joy,
it just comes.
When I try to grasp it,
the mind is no longer joyful
because the self desires to have it.
The joy is like fish in the pond.
Let it be and enjoy seeing her swim.

Silhouette

Light in the darkness is truly bright.
Joy in the midst of suffering is truly sweet.
Joy without suffering is like light without darkness.

Opportunity

Accept difficulties with joy
because difficulty always comes with opportunity.
Joy is the impetus that turns one into the other.

Progress

Progress comes only from change.
When you resist, conflicts occur.
Progress is an effect of change,
of growth that sprouts through resistance.

Happiness

Happiness is a daily practice,
a practice of wise choices.

~ ~

Having it all

The increase of happiness
is proportionate to the decrease of the wants.

Accumulation of happiness

Happiness is a culmination of insight and wisdom.
It's a consequential phenomena of a singleness of being.
Through repetition,
the experiences of happiness accumulate.

Without possession

Happiness is like the water in a little pond.
When you catch it with your hand, it runs away.
Sit and wait, then you see it right in front of your eyes.

No promises

The promise of happiness is a fortress of delusion.

Chapter 7: Fulfillment

The summit

The last step depends upon the first.
The first step depends upon the last.
Keep your eyes fixed on the road to the top
but don't assume that you are there
just because you see the summit.

A rising sun

A new day begins with a rising sun,
the sun that was buried during the night,
the night that was toasted by the day,
the day that comes with new hope,
the hope of anticipation.

No risk

Where there are no obstacles,
there is no opportunity.
Progression through the obstacles
unfolds many hidden treasures.
The more pressured we are,
the higher we can soar.

Limitless

We must realize that neither our greatest fears
nor our greatest hopes are
beyond the limits of our power.
With our patience and determination,
we are eventually able to conquer the fears
and to achieve the hopes.

Imagination

Imagination is a reflective faculty
that takes us out of the body
and travels beyond the space and time.

Opportunity

Quickly take advantage of opportunities when they appear.
They won't last until you figure out what they really are,
because all opportunities come as raw materials
not as finished products that you wish.

Timing

If time is gold,
timing is diamond.

To win

Know your weakness not to lose.
Know your strength to triumph.

Adversity

Struggle is a flow.
A flow of a large river,
a flow of a giant water fall,
a flow of a sweeping valley,
a flow of a small spring brook,
a flow of a early morning pond,
a flow of wild cats.
To escape
know the flow
and create a reverse rhythm.

Transcendence

To win, read the rhythm and ride the force.
To win, create the rhythm for the opponent to follow.
To win without engagement, transcend them all.

The eye of the hurricane

In activity, there must be calmness.
In calmness, there must be activity.
The activity and calmness
are different shadows of the same being.
The calmness is nothing but the activity.

To succeed

Know your capacity,
assess what must be done to succeed,
then adjust your path to the goal
by expanding yourself and condensing the situation.

Greatness

To be great,
whatever you do, do your best.
Be totally attentive to things you do
so that your awareness
can penetrate the essence of things.

One day

Behind the pitch dark White mountain
a dawn crawls down the hills.
The agony of the night is driven
by the rays of the dawn,
the golden rays of the rising sun.
The shadow of the night will haunt me again.
But till the sun is gone
the White mountain shines.

Chapter 8: Wisdom

The wise

The art of listening
is that which makes the wise wiser.

Wisdom

Wisdom is a light in a dark chamber.
The light that clears the darkness
and illuminates all that is.

Water of wisdom

Water shows its essence by holding things together.
Without water,
dry flour makes no bread
and a tree has no shape.
Without water,
our body could be dead dry pieces of soil.

The power of two

Contrast empowers the meaning of two.
Neither excludes nor includes the other.
They are simply coexistent.
Without one, the other finds no place to be.

Knowledge

Knowledge has two sources,
one is acquired,
the other is self-awakened.
The balance of the two armors us with true power.

The garden

The mind is a garden,
confined in a certain space and time
that can be contemplated only from where I am.

Possibility of the other

The light can only shine in the darkness.
The darkness can only be seen in the light.
One is the possibility of the other.

Illumination

Happy is the man who has the power to think, to decide,
to believe, to act, to speak, to read, to see,
to write things that can change life in meaningful ways.

Torch in the darkness

Wisdom is a torch in the darkness.
It lightens the mind so we can see clearly
both the content and process of our becoming.

Grasp what is

A direct grasp of what is right here before my eyes
is the best thing I can do to form the future.
Without it the future has no ground to be.

The summit

I am climbing the path high above the ocean
of which the view is blocked by the cliffs and clouds.
And suddenly through the clouds I see the summit
and take a deep breath.

Difference

We are all different from each other.
We are all born totally independent,
but we are same in pursuit of the quality of our being.

Insight

Insight is invisible.
Insight is nonphysical.
It is a sight with no sight,
an observation with no observer.

The cricket

One hot summer noon
a cricket plops into the sun
dancing in the space.

Song of wisdom

In the autumn woods
An acorn falls
"Ouch !"

調

Chapter 9: Harmony

Changes

The truth is that everything changes.
The flower blossoms and the fruit falls.
Spring comes, the weeds grow.
A life born is destined to die.
In the midst of the uncertainty of changes,
I find need for perfect harmony.
Just let it in, let it go.

Harmony is here

The art of harmony is always at our hands.
It is neither after we learn the art nor before we learn it.
The harmony always is.

No way out

The true art of harmony is just a blank milestone.
It's just a reminder of no way out but the way.

Do nothing

Doing nothing allows us to achieve so much.
Things, otherwise, can never be done.

Mastery of life

A mastery of life is in harmony,
the balance between doing and becoming.
Doing things actively and becoming inactively.
Achieving by doing and arriving by becoming.
If achieving is a human plan,
arriving is the Way.

Peace after the storm

With no troubles, there is no harmony.
Without obstacles, we have no ground to stand on today.
Suffering is the rain that hardens the ground.
Without that firmness, we cannot build a house upon it.

Chaos

After war, follows peace.
After chaos, comes order.
After disease, health is appreciated.
After suffering, there comes balance.

Harmony

Harmony is to be
with the rhythm of every moment.

Peace

The most peaceful time of my life is
when I write about peace.

Sound of silence

When the pond is tranquil,
it reflects the Heaven.
When our mind is still,
it mirrors the Heaven within ourselves.
The sound of silence,
the music of the Heaven.

Silence

Sound arises from the silence.
Sound returns to the silence.
Silence is an eternal being,
sound a phenomenon.
No silence, no sound.

Solitude

Solitude is the true identity of self.
The self was born alone and is going to leave alone.
To get comfortable with it, is to understand the self.
Then life becomes less burdensome.

Magic

When my mind is in complete silence, magic happens.
My house, books, pictures, and my family
as well as myself disappear.
All are gone.
Happiness is gone.
Problems are gone.
Yesterday is gone.
Tomorrow is gone.
And, most of all, time stops.

Now

The moment that we live,
this moment right here,
is the only proof of our existence.
Without this moment
everything must be sucked into the vacant hole of
darkness.

Relativity

Harmony is relative experience.
Even though small things are in harmony,
the whole cannot be.
Even though small things are not in harmony,
the whole can be.